Decorating

EASTER EGGS

By Mara
Reid Rogers

Photographs
by Mark Hill

Little, Brown and Company
Boston New York Toronto London

Dedication

This book is dedicated to all children. May you always be inspired to create, and, like Jack in "Jack and the Beanstalk," may you never be short of music or of golden eggs.

First Edition

ISBN 0-316-75414-5

10 9 8 7 6 5 4 3 2 1

Published simultaneously in Canada by Little, Brown & Company (Canada) Limited

Not recommended for children under three years of age

Printed and bound in China

About the author and photographer

Mara Reid Rogers has written several cookbooks, two of which have photographs by her husband, photographer Mark Hill. This is her first children's book. She and her husband live with their two feline-children, Sam and Misha, in Atlanta, Georgia.

Mark Hill is a studio and still-life photographer with a great sense of humor. His work has appeared in *Bon Appétit*, *Cosmopolitan*, and the *New York Times Magazine*, among other publications.

 Contents

Getting Ready and Getting Started

MATERIALS

Ready to decorate? Here is a list of the materials that you'll find in the craft kit that comes packaged with this book:

18 egg dye tablets in plum purple, sky blue, tomato red, sunshine yellow, tropical orange, and spring green (3 of each color)

44 fun stickers

1 sheet of sparkling press-on jewels

A rainbow of 50 fluffy feathers in electric blue, egg-yolk yellow, grass green, deep purple, bubble-gum pink, and rose red

Dazzling silver glitter

Glitzy gold glitter

1 red egg dipper

1 purple egg drying stand

To complete the projects, you'll also need a few additional items, most of which should be readily available around your house or can be purchased from a crafts supply store. These additional elements are listed at the start of each project.

PREPARING YOUR EGGS

The best way to get your eggs ready for decorating is to blow the insides out of the shells. This will allow you to keep your masterpieces for as long as you want. If you don't want to blow out the eggs, you can have a parent help you hard-boil them—but you will have to refrigerate them, and they will only keep for about three days.

Most of the projects in the book can be made with either blown or hard-boiled eggs. The Marble Egg Masterpiece, Pirate's Treasure, Polly the Parrot, Pocketful of Posies, and Stained Glass Window egg, however, can be made only with blown eggs.

How to Blow Out an Egg

Cover your work surface with some old newspapers to protect it. Place a medium-sized bowl on the newspapers, and hold a large raw white egg over the bowl. With the point of a large safety pin, carefully poke a hole in the top of the egg, being careful not to crack the rest of its shell. Turn the egg over, and poke a second hole in its bottom.

Make the top hole larger by carefully moving the safety pin around in a circular motion until the hole is about ⅛ of an inch wide. Repeat the process with the bottom hole, making it slightly larger than the top hole. Be sure to puncture the egg's inner white membrane at both ends. The egg will blow out even more easily if you puncture its yolk with a toothpick.

Still holding the egg over the bowl, put the top end of the egg (the one with the smaller hole) to your mouth, and blow. (If you want, you can hold the end of a plastic drinking straw firmly against the smaller, top hole, and blow through that. This sometimes makes it easier to blow out the contents.) The egg white and yolk will be blown out of the eggshell and into the bowl through the larger, lower hole, leaving a hollow eggshell. (Save the eggs and use them to make scrambled eggs or French toast. Just cover the bowl with plastic wrap or pour the eggs into a lidded plastic container, and refrigerate.)

Run a slow stream of cold water through the hollow egg to rinse it out. Let the empty eggshell dry on the egg drying stand from the kit for about one hour before dyeing or decorating it. Be sure to handle the eggshell with care; it is fragile and can crack easily.

How to Dye an Egg with Egg Dye Tablets from the Kit

Cover your work surface with old newspapers to protect it. Pour 1 tablespoon of white vinegar into a small nonplastic bowl (as the dye tends to stain plastic). Add one dye tablet from the craft kit. Using a metal tablespoon, stir until the tablet is dissolved. Add ½ cup cold water and stir until well blended.

Using the egg dipper from the kit, lower the egg into the dye bath. Pull it up with the egg dipper after two minutes or so to see if it's achieved the color you want. The longer you keep the egg in the dye, the darker the color will be.

If you are dyeing a blown egg, it may keep

popping up out of the water, because it is hollow. Keep turning it and putting it under the water with your egg dipper so that it will take the dye color evenly. Often, the inside of the egg will become filled with water and the egg will then stay underwater.

Drain a blown egg by tipping it with the egg dipper over the dye bath; a hard-boiled egg should be gently blotted on a paper towel. Place your egg on the stand until it is completely dry (about one hour).

How to Dye an Egg with Food Coloring

Cover your work surface with old newspapers to protect it. Pour ½ cup boiling water and 1 teaspoon white vinegar into a small nonplastic bowl. Gently squeeze 20 drops of food coloring into the water, and stir with a metal tablespoon until well blended. If you want a lighter color, use less food coloring; for a darker shade, use more food coloring.

Using the egg dipper from the kit, lower the egg into the dye bath, and dye it as described for the dye tablets until it is the color you want. Drain the egg well or gently blot it on a paper towel. Then let it dry completely on the egg stand (about one hour).

You may have an egg that will not take the color no matter how long it sits in the bath. This is because a coating of oil is sometimes sprayed on eggs. Try doubling the white vinegar in the dye bath to 2 tablespoons for the tablets or 2 teaspoons for the food coloring; the dye should then take better. If it doesn't, dye another egg, and decorate the one that wouldn't dye with glitter, paint, or some other material.

Food Color Mixing Guide

Most food coloring sets come with four different colors: red, blue, green, and yellow. It is very easy to create other colors from these basic four. Just follow these formulas:

> **Orange = 6 drops red + 14 drops yellow**
> **Turquoise = 15 drops blue + 5 drops green**
> **Purple = 10 drops red + 4 drops blue**

How to Glue-Wash and Glitter-Dust an Egg

Use this technique *only* with blown eggs. First cover your work surface with old newspapers to protect it. To make enough glue wash for one egg, combine 3 teaspoons white glue with 1½ teaspoons water in a small glass bowl and stir with a plastic spoon until well blended. Using a medium tipped paintbrush, "paint" the egg with the glue wash until it has a thin, even coat all over.

Transfer the wet glue-washed egg to a small self-sealing plastic bag filled with 1 tablespoon of the glitter of your choice. Seal the bag and gently shake it. The glitter will stick to the glue-washed egg. Continue shaking until the egg has an even layer of glitter coating. Carefully transfer the egg to the egg stand and let it dry completely (for about two hours) before decorating it. Wash your brush and glass bowl right away, before the glue wash dries.

How to Glaze Your Decorated Egg

Use this technique *only* with blown eggs. You can give your finished egg project a shiny, glossy look by painting it with a thin coat of clear shellac (following the package directions) or colorless nail polish. Be sure to ask your mom or dad to help.

How to Make an Egg Holder

If you want your finished egg project to stand up, then use some all-purpose white glue to attach it to one of the following:

Toothpaste cap (Glue egg to smaller end)

Screw-off plastic soda-bottle cap

Napkin ring (Ask your mom or dad if it is okay to use this)

Make sure to let the glue dry for at least twenty-four hours.

Humpty Dumpty's Batik Buddy

When you draw on an egg with crayons and then dye it, the design you drew doesn't disappear. Like magic, it reappears after you bring the egg out of the dye bath. This process is called batik.

WHAT YOU NEED

- Light blue, yellow, dark blue, and red wax crayons
- Blown or hard-boiled white egg
- Sunshine yellow dye tablet (from kit) or yellow food coloring

1. With the light blue crayon, draw a small bow-tie design on the egg.

2. Using the yellow crayon, draw another bow-tie design perpendicular to the blue bow tie, so that the two designs form a circle. Continue this pattern, drawing additional bow-tie circles around the egg ¼ of an inch apart, alternating between the light blue and yellow and the dark blue and red crayons.

3. Follow the instructions on pages 5–6 to dye the egg yellow. Gently place the egg on the egg stand and allow it to dry for two hours. If you want Humpty Dumpty's Batik Buddy to have a glossy appearance, follow the instructions on page 7 to give it a shiny glaze.

VARIATION:
To make a turtle: Make the egg according to the project directions, but dye the egg green instead of yellow. Using bright green non-hardening modeling clay, form one small ball (for the head), four smaller balls (for the feet), and one very small sausage-shaped piece (for the tail).

To form the head, press the largest ball against the tip of the egg so that it sticks. Using a toothpick, make one hole on either side of the head to form eyes. Press the four smaller balls onto the egg to form the turtle's feet, then press one end of the sausage-shaped piece of clay onto the egg to form the tail.

Feelin' Groovy Tie-Dye Egg

This finished egg may look hard to make, but you'll be surprised at how easy it is. After you've completed the egg shown here, try experimenting by wrapping the rubber bands in a random pattern around a white egg for some more amazing effects!

WHAT YOU NEED

- Blown or hard-boiled white egg colored with the sunshine yellow dye tablet (from kit) or yellow food coloring (see pages 5–6 for instructions)
- 2 thin medium-sized rubber bands (green in photo)
- 2 thin small rubber bands (red in photo)
- Tomato red dye tablet (from kit) or red food coloring
- Spring green dye tablet (from kit) or green food coloring

1. Loop the two medium-sized rubber bands around the yellow-dyed egg to form a cross. (Make sure they are not twisted but lie flat.) Wrap the two small rubber bands around the egg in a diagonal cross that intersects the first cross at the center. Again, make sure the rubber bands are not twisted but lie flat.

2. Make a red dye bath, following the instructions on pages 5–6. Then follow the dyeing instructions—but you're going to dye only half of the egg red, by dipping the egg lengthwise into the dye bath until it reaches the bottom edge of the rubber band that divides the egg in half lengthwise.

After it is sufficiently dyed, gently blot the egg with a paper towel and transfer it to the drying stand. Allow it to dry for about two hours.

VARIATION:
To make a graffiti egg:
Follow step 1. Then, before
you proceed with step 2,
write words like *peace*, *love*,
joy, or whatever you like in
between the rubber bands
with a white crayon.

3. Make a green dye bath, following the instructions on pages 5–6. Follow the procedure described in step 2 to dye the other side of the egg green.

Gently blot the egg with a paper towel, transfer it to the drying stand, and allow it to dry for about two hours.

When the egg is completely dry, carefully remove the rubber bands one by one, so as to avoid cracking or breaking the egg.

The Secret Garden

The next time you play outside or go to the park, gather some leaves, ferns, grass, and small flowers to make this decorative natural egg. It will remind you that with Easter comes spring!

WHAT YOU NEED

- An old pair of panty hose

- A few freshly picked leaves, ferns, spears of grass, and/or small flowers (Gather small leaves with interesting shapes. They may be from houseplants, weeds, or very young trees. Be careful about gathering leaves outdoors, though—stay away from poison ivy or poison oak!)

- Blown or hard-boiled white egg

- Twist tie (from box of plastic sandwich bags or garbage bags)

- Small bowl

- Spring green dye tablet (from kit) or green food coloring

1. Cut a 4-inch square from an old pair of panty hose. Lay the square piece of panty hose on a work surface. Arrange a few fresh leaves or flowers on the panty hose square, and carefully place the egg on top of them.

2. Gently gather the panty hose around the egg, pulling it up so that the panty hose stretches over the plants as tightly as possible. It is important that you see the plants and egg through the panty hose mesh. Tie the twist tie around the panty hose where it is bunched together, and twist it until it is tightly secured. (You will use the twist tie as a handle when you dye the egg.)

3. Follow the instructions on pages 5–6 to dye the egg spring green. Hold the twist tie to dip the egg into the dye bath so that your hands don't get wet. Gently place the panty-hose-wrapped egg on the egg stand, and allow it to dry for at least eight hours, preferably overnight.

4. When the egg and panty hose are completely dry, undo the twist tie, unwrap the egg, and gently remove the plants to reveal your Secret Garden! If you'd like your Secret Garden egg to have a shiny appearance, follow the instructions on page 7 to give it a glaze.

VARIATION:
For a two-tone egg: Before you wrap the egg with the plants and panty hose, dye it any light color (following the dyeing instructions on pages 5–6). Let it dry, then proceed with the project instructions, using a darker color for the second dye. This way, your plants will appear in the light color.

Polly the Parrot

After you've created your own Polly the Parrot, take a piece of double-sided tape, or double over a piece of masking tape, and place it under the cork "pads" of Polly's feet: Then she'll be able to stand on your desk, bedside table, or any flat surface.

WHAT YOU NEED

- Scissors
- Sheet of brown construction paper or other heavyweight paper
- Cork (from a bottle or a crafts store)
- Fine-point black marker
- All-purpose white glue
- Sheet of yellow construction paper or other heavyweight paper
- Blown white egg colored with the sunshine yellow dye tablet (from kit) or yellow food coloring
- Yellow bird-eye stickers (from kit) or colored marker
- 3 egg-yolk yellow feathers (from kit)
- 2 rose red feathers (from kit)
- 1 deep purple feather (from kit)

VARIATION:

To make a person: Assemble the egg up through step 2, but do not draw lines for claws. Instead of a beak, cut lips out of red construction paper and ears from pink construction paper, or use a marker to draw lips and ears. Use the human eye stickers from the kit, or draw your own. Insert a shortened purple head feather for hair. Then finish by completing step 6.

1. Cut two triangles with 1¾-inch-long sides from brown construction paper. These triangles will be Polly's feet. Ask an adult to help you cut with a knife two ⅛-inch-thick slices from the bottle cork. These will be the pads for Polly's feet.

2. Using a black marker, draw three short lines (for claws), 1/16 of an inch apart and side by side, on one point of each of the triangle feet. Glue each foot to a piece of cork. Squeeze a tiny dot of glue on a side corner of one triangle. Then place a side corner of the second triangle on top of it so that the two triangles overlap slightly and stick together.

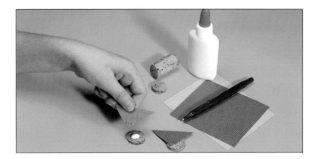

3. Cut a triangle with two ¾-inch-long sides and one 1-inch-long side from yellow construction paper. This will be Polly's beak. Fold the beak in half. Squeeze a very fine line of glue on the edge of the beak and gently press it against the yellow-dyed egg.

4. Press the two parrot eye stickers from the kit onto the egg above the beak, or use a marker to draw your own.

5. Very gently push the hard ends of three yellow feathers into the bottom hole in the egg. These will be Polly's tail feathers. Angle the feathers so that they point upward, bending them slightly if necessary. Do the same with two red feathers.

6. Squeeze some glue onto the feet where they overlap. Lower the parrot body onto the feet, and hold it until it sticks. Lean the parrot body against a stack of books so that it can stand upright, undisturbed, while it dries, which will take about four hours.

7. To finish the parrot, gently insert the purple feather into the egg's top hole to make a head feather.

Pirate's Treasure

By using items from around the house, along with sparkling gold glitter and fancy jewels from the craft kit, you can make this spectacular egg for yourself or a special friend! It looks as if it was washed ashore as part of the loot from a pirate's treasure chest.

WHAT YOU NEED

- Scissors
- Small white doilies or colorful gift wrap
- Gold glitter-dusted blown egg (see page 7 for instructions)

- All-purpose white glue
- Press-on jewels (from kit) or colorful plastic beads
- Narrow gold ribbon, braid, or rickrack

1. Using scissors, cut several small circles from a doily or gift-wrap paper.

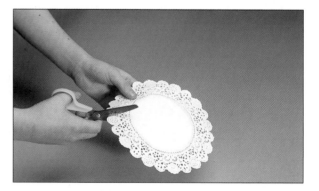

2. Glue a circle onto the gold egg, pressing firmly until it lies flat and smooth. Repeat this with your other circles. Once your circles have dried, you can decorate the egg by pressing on the jewels from the kit or by gluing on some plastic beads.

3. Draw a thin line of glue lengthwise down each side of the egg. Firmly press the ribbon, braid, or rickrack in place until it sticks to the egg. Using scissors, cut off any excess ribbon, trimming the ends so that they meet but do not overlap. Set the egg aside to dry for about two hours.

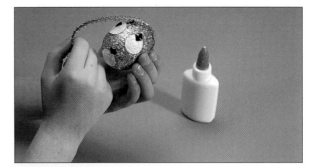

VARIATION:
Replace the doily circles with small circles cut from aluminum foil that have been wadded up into tiny balls. Finish your egg with silver ribbon instead of gold.

Sally at the Seashore

When you make the Sally at the Seashore egg, you'll not only have fun, but you'll be able to use all of those pebbles and seashells that you've collected on the beach. You can even trade seashells and pebbles with your friends so that you have a large selection to choose from!

WHAT YOU NEED

- Sand from the beach (or colored sand from a crafts store)
- Medium-sized bowl
- Blown or hard-boiled white egg colored with the sky blue dye tablet (from kit) or blue food coloring
- All-purpose white glue
- Tiny pebbles and seashells (from the beach or a crafts store)
- Cork (from a bottle or a crafts store) broken into small pieces
- Seashore stickers (from kit)

1. Pour the sand into the bowl. Then carefully squeeze a small amount of glue onto the egg in a wave design.

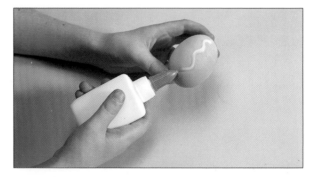

2. Working quickly before the glue dries, hold the egg over the bowl and lightly sprinkle some sand onto the waves. Continue this process until the waves are covered evenly with the sand. Gently blow on the sand waves so that any excess sand falls into the bowl. Place the egg on the egg stand to dry for about two hours.

3. Decorate your egg by gluing the pebbles, seashells, and pieces of cork onto it and by pressing on stickers from the craft kit.

VARIATION:
Instead of using stickers, cut out abstract shapes from patterned fabrics or wrapping paper and decorate your egg with them.

Stained Glass Window

This fancy egg takes a little patience to make, but the results are worth it! If you do not already have some colored cellophane paper at home, you can find it at most crafts supply stores.

WHAT YOU NEED

- Blown white egg
- Heavenly body stickers (from kit)
- Scissors
- 2 different colors of cellophane paper
- All-purpose white glue
- Fine-point permanent black marker
- 6-inch length of narrow ribbon (optional)
- Small paper clip (optional)

1. Decorate your white egg with a sticker.

2. Using your scissors, cut out four small triangles from each of the two colors of cellophane paper. Each triangle should have sides that are about ¾ of an inch long.

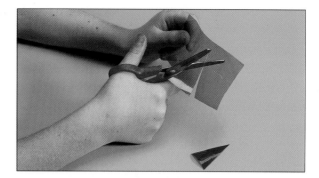

3. Squeeze a tiny drop of glue onto each of the three points of a cellophane paper triangle. Lay the triangle, glue side down, over the sticker, so that the sticker falls in the center of the triangle. Gently press the triangle so that it sticks to the egg and lies flat and smooth.

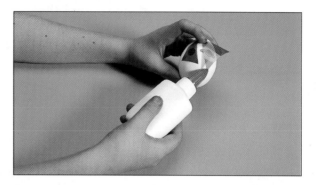

4. Repeat this process with other stickers (leaving large spaces in between each sticker) and cellophane paper triangles until the whole egg is covered with a single layer of triangles. You may need to cut out additional cellophane triangles if you run out before your egg is completely covered. Alternate the colors, overlapping the edges slightly and turning the triangles in different directions.

5. Using a black marker, gently draw thin lines to outline each triangle, even when it overlaps another triangle. This will help give the illusion of the leaded-glass panes of a stained glass window.

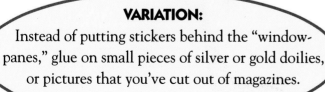

VARIATION:
Instead of putting stickers behind the "windowpanes," glue on small pieces of silver or gold doilies, or pictures that you've cut out of magazines.

6. If you want to hang up your Stained Glass Window egg, ask an adult to help you very carefully cut away any cellophane paper covering the top blowhole. Then make a small loop in one end of a piece of narrow ribbon and tie a knot at the opposite end. Hook a small paper clip into the knot, and very carefully insert the paper clip into the top hole of the egg. Gently tug on the ribbon until the paper clip is sideways in the egg and holds the ribbon loop securely. ·

Marvelous Mosaic

In this project you make two batches of salt dough, which is enough to decorate about six eggs, perfect for an Easter egg decorating party! But if you're going to make only one egg, save any leftover dough for future use. Place each color in a separate self-sealing plastic bag, squeeze out all the air from each bag, and seal. Store up to one week at room temperature.

WHAT YOU NEED

For one batch of salt dough, combine the following ingredients in a medium bowl:

🥚 ¾ cup all-purpose flour

🥚 ½ cup salt

🥚 ⅓ cup water mixed with 15 drops of food coloring

🥚 1 tablespoon silver glitter (from kit)

You will need to make two batches of salt dough so that you will have two different colors of dough.

🥚 2 large self-sealing plastic bags

🥚 Blown or hard-boiled white egg

1. ◆ Combine the ingredients for one batch of dough in a medium-sized bowl. Stir until well blended. Transfer the dough to one of the plastic bags, and seal it closed. Repeat the process for a second batch of dough, choosing a different color.

2. ◆ Knead each batch of dough by squeezing the dough with your hands through the closed bag until it is well blended and smooth.

3. Working with one batch of dough at a time, pinch off a small piece of dough and roll it between your fingers to form a tiny ball. Repeat this step until you have about fifty balls of each of the two colors of dough. (If the dough is too crumbly to work with, add a little water to the bag and knead the dough until it is workable. If the dough is too sticky, add a little flour to the bag and knead it until it is workable.)

4. Press a dough ball onto the egg. Gently flatten the ball with your index finger to begin your mosaic pattern. Continue to make and press dough balls side by side onto the egg, alternating the colors until the egg is entirely covered with a pattern of your choice. (Wash and dry your hands in between working with each color, so that the colors don't come off on each other.)

5. Gently place the egg on the egg stand, and set it aside to dry for about twelve hours. Turn the egg over and set it back on the egg stand. Set it aside for another twelve hours, or until the salt dough has completely dried and hardened.

VARIATION:
For a more glittery appearance: Glaze your finished mosaic egg following the directions on page 7. While the glaze is still wet, sprinkle some glitter on your egg. Then set it on the egg stand to dry for about four hours. For a really colorful egg: Make four different batches of colored dough.

Very Veggie

Carrots from the fridge, uncooked pasta from the cupboards, and an ordinary pencil become printing blocks to make this simple but kaleidoscopic egg. Just "ink" the blocks with some poster paints and you're ready to go!

WHAT YOU NEED

- 2 large carrots
- Blunt, dull dinner knife
- 4 cotton swabs
- 4 different colors of nontoxic poster paint

- Blown or hard-boiled white egg
- 1 new eraser-topped pencil
- 1 piece of interestingly shaped dried pasta, such as rigatoni (which is tube-shaped)
- Flower and butterfly stickers (from kit)

1. Ask an adult to help you trim off the tip of a carrot and cut out a small, flat raised triangle from its face. Do the same with the second carrot, but instead of a triangle, cut a small, flat raised square. These will be two of your "printing blocks."

2. Dip a cotton swab into one color of poster paint, then dab the paint onto the carrot triangle. Press the carrot gently against the egg to print a triangle. Repeat the process as often as desired to create a pattern, "re-inking" the triangle in between prints.

3. Applying the same technique, print squares (using the carrot with the square cut in it), circles (using the eraser on the top of the pencil), and loops (using the end of the piece of pasta). Print each shape using a different color.

4. Gently place the egg on the egg stand and allow it to dry for about four hours. If you want the Very Veggie egg to have a glossy appearance, follow the instructions on page 7 to give it a shiny glaze after it has dried.

5. When the egg is completely dry, press some flower and butterfly stickers from the kit onto it.

VARIATION:
Instead of decorating your egg with stickers, glue on bright and festive confetti. To make confetti, use a hole punch to make tiny dots from comic strips, magazines, or construction paper.

Cabbage Patch Bunny

Here is a bunny caught in your vegetable garden. But you probably won't mind if he nibbles your carrots and cabbage, because he's so cute!

WHAT YOU NEED

- Scissors
- New dry sponge
- 2 cotton swabs
- Pink and purple nontoxic poster paint
- Blown or hard-boiled white egg

- Pink bunny-eye stickers or blue human-eye stickers (from kit) or colored marker
- Sheet of pink construction paper or other heavy-weight paper
- All-purpose white glue
- 1 piece of thin dried spaghetti
- 1 small pink plastic bead
- White cotton ball
- 2 flat dried white lima beans (or buttons)

1. Cut two ¾-inch-wide circles from the sponge.

2. Using a cotton swab, spread some pink poster paint on one of the sponge circles and gently press the sponge, paint side down, against the white egg. Repeat the process as often as desired to create a pattern, spreading the sponge with the paint in between prints.

Bunny Ear Pattern

3. Print some purple circles with the second sponge circle and purple poster paint. Gently place the egg on the egg stand, and allow it to dry for about four hours.

4. When the egg is dry, press the two bunny-eye or human-eye stickers onto the egg, or use a marker to draw your own eyes.

5. Cut two bunny ears about 3 inches long from pink construction paper, following the drawing on the opposite page. Bend the square end of each ear back slightly to make a tab. Glue each ear tab to the top of the egg above the eyes.

6. Cut two 2-inch-long pieces of dried spaghetti. Place a drop of glue inside the bead and insert both pieces of spaghetti to form an X. These will be your bunny's whiskers.

7. Glue the bead with the spaghetti whiskers below the eyes. Lay the bunny down on its side to dry undisturbed for about four hours.

8. Using a marker, draw the bunny's smile and two teeth. Glue on a cotton ball for its tail. Place the two dried beans or buttons side by side and squeeze a drop of glue in between them. These will be the bunny's feet. Squeeze a drop of glue on top where they meet, then hold until the glue dries. Hold the bunny body onto the feet until it sticks. Lean the bunny against a stack of books so that it can stand upright, undisturbed, while it dries, which will take about four hours.

VARIATION:
To make a tiger: Assemble the egg according to the directions, but decorate it with orange and black sponge prints. Use an orange bead for a nose, and cut out triangle ears from orange construction paper. Leave off the cotton tail, but glue on a long tail cut from orange construction paper on which you have drawn black stripes.

Pocketful of Posies

Here is a project that makes a great gift for your mom or grandmother on Mother's Day. Since these flowers are made from feathers, they will never wilt! You can make just a single flower, but it's nice to make more than one in different colors to fill an entire vase.

WHAT YOU NEED

- Blown white egg colored with the tropical orange dye tablet (from kit) or orange-blended food coloring

- Press-on jewels (from kit) or colorful plastic beads

- All-purpose white glue

- 2 egg-yolk yellow feathers (from kit)

- 4 electric blue feathers (from kit)

- 2 grass green feathers (from kit)

- 1 green pipe cleaner

1. Create a pattern of press-on jewels on the tip of the orange egg, or glue on some plastic beads.

2. Glue the two yellow feather "petals" opposite each other on the egg, followed by the four blue feather "petals."

3. Glue the two green feather "leaves" two-thirds of the way up the pipe cleaner. Insert the pipe cleaner into the bottom hole of the egg to make a stem.

4. While holding the egg, gently bend the upper part of the pipe cleaner slightly downward so that you can see into the flower. Put your "flower" into a bottle or vase, and let it dry upright for three hours.

VARIATION:
For a fragrant flower: Before dyeing your egg, ask your mom or dad for a tiny drop of perfume or cologne to put into the colored dye bath. Make several perfumed flowers in different colors for a lovely—and lovely-smelling—bouquet.

Marble Egg Masterpiece

Remember that last field trip you took to the art museum? Can't you imagine this majestic egg as part of the exhibition?

WHAT YOU NEED

- Square cardboard box, with a lid at least 4 inches by 4 inches
- Thin 2¼-inch-long nail with medium-sized head
- Blown white egg
- Magenta, purple, and orange nontoxic poster paints
- All-purpose white glue
- 3 small glass bowls
- 3 plastic spoons
- Medium-point paintbrush
- Cotton swab

This is the most difficult project in the book. You may need an adult's help.

1. Ask an adult to help you make a handling rack. Insert the nail point first through the closed box, leaving 2 inches of nail showing above. Lower the egg onto the nail, bottom end first, until the nail head reaches the interior top of the egg and the egg bottom almost rests on top of the box lid. Be sure to use a blown egg with a small top blowhole, so the nail won't slip through the top of the egg. Since the wet egg will be very slippery and difficult to handle, this rack will hold the egg still while you are working on it.

2. To make the magenta "glue paint" for the background of your egg, combine 1 tablespoon glue and 1 teaspoon magenta poster paint in a bowl. Then combine 2 teaspoons glue and ¼ teaspoon purple poster paint in a second bowl, and 2 teaspoons glue and ¼ teaspoon orange poster paint in a third bowl. Using the three plastic spoons, stir each glue-paint mixture until it is well blended.

3. Using the brush, gently paint the magenta glue-paint in a thin, even layer all over the egg. Don't worry if it drips on the box. Do *not* let the egg dry; continue with the next steps while the egg is still wet.

4. Using the plastic spoon, drop about ½ teaspoon purple glue-paint on top of the egg. Then drop about ½ teaspoon orange glue-paint next to the purple paint. Repeat this twice, so that you end with six alternating color drips on top of the egg. Let the paint drip down the side of the egg.

5. Slowly and gently pull the cotton swab head across and through the color drips. Continue around the entire egg, being careful not to knock the egg off the nail. This motion will create a swirling pattern that looks like marble. Continue this process until you have created a marble pattern over the entire egg.

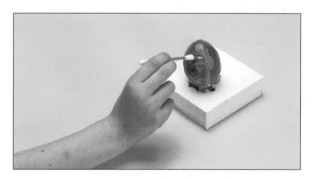

6. Let the egg dry on the holding rack for twenty-four hours (the egg can't dry on the egg stand because it will stick to it).

When the egg is thoroughly dry, very gently lift it up and off the nail, and discard the box. If you want the egg to have a glossy appearance, follow the instructions on page 7 to give it a shiny glaze.

VARIATION:
For a more complicated project but an
extremely impressive egg, drip a third color of glue
paint onto the egg!